Indoor gardening

Leslie Johns

Edited for U.S. Houseplant Fanciers
By Marjorie Dietz

Pocket
Gardener

Floraprint

Published 1977 by Floraprint Limited,
Park Road, Calverton, Nottingham.
Designed and produced for Floraprint by
Intercontinental Book Productions
Copyright © 1977 Intercontinental Book Productions
and Floraprint Limited. North American edition Copy-
right © 1981 Intercontinental Book Productions and
Floraprint U.S.A.

ISBN 0-938804-02-2

Design by Design Practitioners Limited

Photographs supplied by Floraprint Limited (copyright
I.G.A.), Leslie Johns and Associates, Harry Smith,
Syndication International and DP Press Limited.

Cover photograph supplied by Harry Smith

Printed in U.S.A.

Contents

1 Indoor plants

Plant requirements

Our needs, and those of the indoor plants we try to grow, are very similar. Food, water, light, warmth, cleanliness and shelter are essential to us both and we flourish only when we get the exact degree of each we need. Plants are exactly like their owners. They resist hard and fast rules, respond to individual treatment and differ just as humans do.

But there is more to cultivating plants than this. For example, if two identical plants were bought on the same day in the same city and taken home to seemingly identical houses, one could be dead in a week while the other thrived in spite of the fact that each owner followed what he or she considered to be the same directions for plant care. Different conditions in the two homes could be a contributory factor, one house being warmer, lighter, cleaner and more humid than the other. But the main cause is more likely to be the owner's individual interpretation of the instructions. What does the recommendation 'water lightly' mean to you? Once a day? Once a week? By the teaspoon? Or by the cup? Although the best guide is undoubtedly experience, it is possible to get a rough idea of the cultural requirements of most plants simply by looking at them and perhaps by knowing something of their families.

We can all recognize cacti, for example; they are unmistakable, and most people know that they like as much sun as they can get, plenty of water in summer, but little in winter. So if we are given a plant that looks like a cactus, the probability is that if we treat it as such it will thrive.

This is a particularly simple example,

Note that the flowering plants, mainly cyclamen, in this group are nearest to the window light.

but there are other helpful guidelines we can follow. All flowering plants and all with variegated foliage must have good light to retain their vivid colors. The darker green the leaf the less light the plant will need. Only cacti and certain other succulents will flourish in full summer sun. Only cyperus and certain other marginal marsh plants can tolerate having their roots stand in water.

Detailed instructions for the proper care of indoor plants will appear later, but for convenience most plants can be divided into groups with similar tastes or requirements. The cactus group is particularly easy to cater for. Growing in the open, away from meadows, hills and forests, they are consequently accustomed to the full glare of the sun. So, if we pick out other plants that normally grow in the open, the chances are that they, too, like cacti, will require full sun. Pelargoniums, or common geraniums, love the sun. So do nearly all the succulents, echeveria, kalanchoe, sansevieria, aloe,

Nearly all rebutias are spherical like these and all are among the 'easier' cacti in terms of flowering.

Agave leaves are sharply pointed and saw-edged, so plants should be given plenty of space indoors. *Agave franzosinii* 'Aurea' is easy to grow and long-lived if kept in light, warm conditions.

agave, crassula, sempervivum and the like. These may not be quite so immediately recognizable as cacti, but practically without exception they have thick, fleshy leaves that are capable of absorbing and storing quantities of moisture on which the plants can live during the dry season. All these plants need generous supplies of water in the summer and when they flower, but if they continue to receive the same quantities of water in the cooler months of their resting period, their roots will rot and their leaves or swollen stems will yellow and fall, or alternatively turn soft and slimy. In the cold months some of these plants will actually seem to shrivel, but if you give them more than the smallest drink you will do them more harm than good. Return to regular and plentiful watering only when the plant resumes active growth in full sun. The only real exceptions among the succulents, are the leafy types, epiphyllum, zygocactus and schlumbergera.

Like many succulents, *Aloe spinossissima*, with its prickly leaves, is more interesting than beautiful.

These include the so-called Christmas cactus (*Zygocactus truncatus*) and Easter cactus (*Rhipsalidopsis gaertneri*). They are epiphytes, which grow in their native lands on the topmost branches of forest trees. As such, they demand neither full summer sun nor complete winter drought. They can stand both full sun and drought for a time but neither indefinitely.

Apart from cacti and other succulents, most indoor plants need good light away from full sun, and dryer soil conditions in winter than in summer.

As a general rule, the requirements of one species of a genus, will tend to be similar to those of its fellow species in the same group. Some of the most useful, robust and easily available of all indoor plants are the true ivies (*Hedera*), the figs and rubber plants (*Ficus*), and the philodendrons. All the ivies, whether green or variegated, whether derived from *Hedera helix* (common ivy) or *H. canariensis* (Canary Island ivy), require much the same treatment, although the variegated kinds keep their color best when in good light. There are a great many varieties, some with minute differences and others that vary widely in leaf color or size. All are excellent, and all are easily grown indoors.

The fig (*Ficus*) is also widely spread. Its most famous variety is probably *Ficus elastica*, the rubber plant, which again is found in many versions, some with different leaf colorations but others merely tougher and easier-to-grow examples of the old species. *F. benjamina*, the weeping fig, will grow just as tall as the rubber plant, but it has smaller, daintier leaves and a rather engaging and elegant drooping growth. The Indian laurel (*F. retusa nitida*) has leaves about the size of the weeping fig, but its growth is decidedly upright. More like the rubber plant is the fiddle-back fig, *F. lyrata* or *F. pandurata*, whose large and somewhat crinkled leaves are shaped much like the body of a fiddle or violin.

Quite different are two creeping or trailing figs, *F. pumila* also known as *F. repens* or

Ficus benjamina is a graceful, tree-like member of the decorative and useful fig family.

F. stipulata, the creeping fig, with small leaves on wiry stems, and *F. radicans 'Variegata',* whose similar small leaves have golden markings on the foliage. Both of these need a little more water than the larger, tree-like examples of the family.

Curiously enough, one of the most useful groups of indoor plants comes from a family that used to be known only for its edible fruit. This is the pineapple, which belongs, with other plants, to an interesting group known as bromeliads. The indoor pineapple is generally more colorful and decorative than the variety that appears on our tables. Striped with green and gold, tinged with pink, and heavily toothed, it is

known as *Ananas bracteatus striatus.* A smaller version and one more suited to most interiors is *A. comosus 'Nanus'.* Most of the bromeliads are epiphytes, growing in their natural habitat on the bark of trees rather than in the soil. Their long, slim leaves radiate from an open center to form a cup or vase, which in the jungle fills with rain water, on which the plants feed while their clinging roots draw sustenance from fallen leaves that catch up around them as they drop. It follows, therefore, that indoor bromeliads will be happy in surprisingly small pots with any soil so long as it is well drained. The plants are watered by keeping the central vase or cup topped up with water in imitation of their natural habit. In many species a flower arises from the center of this cup, sometimes at the end of a long arching spike. Some are strikingly beautiful and others very longlasting.

One of the best known of these bromeliads is probably the Greek vase plant (*Quesnelia maramorata* syn. *Aechmea rhodocyanea*), which has gray-green glaucous foliage from which a long flowering stem protrudes bearing a series of spiky, soft pink bracts from which grow a multitude of tiny pink, blue and violet flowers. These soon fade, but the pink inflorescence will last for two or three months. A similar plant is the silver vase (*Aechmea fasciata*).

Other bromeliads normally grown indoors include neoregelia, nidularium, vriesia, billbergia and cryptanthus.

Another plant that is just as easy to grow, was once very familiar, but has since fallen from fashion is the aspidistra, also known as the parlor-palm or cast-iron plant. Popular in Victorian times largely because it was one of the very few plants that would tolerate dark gaslit rooms warmed by smoky coal fires, *Aspidistra elatior* and the more attractive gold-striped form, *A.e. 'Variegata',* have regained much of their former respectability and are once again in vogue. They are easy to grow and, since they make no particular demands on the indoor gardener, are ideal for the beginner.

It is difficult to convey exactly what an aspidistra plant looks like. To say that the leaves are spear-shaped, about 24 in (70 cm) long and grow arching out from the rhizomatous base on short stems belies its distinctive character. But its general shape is bushy rather than tree-like, trailing or climbing.

Like the aspidistra, the majority of indoor plants have to be classified as bushy because they fit no other category. And there is little one can do to persuade a bushy plant to grow some other way. Some plants can be trained to grow up a wall or along a shelf, but a bushy plant merely occupies a space and bears leaves whose tips are rounded.

Describing a tree-like plant is easier, but to find them indoors is more difficult, for real indoor trees are few. Probably the best known is the familiar India rubber plant, *Ficus elastica*, with some of its relatives, especially the weeping Fig, *F. benjamina*. Less well known, but still a genuine tree, is the cultivated form of the Norfolk Island pine, *Araucaria heterophylla* syn. *excelsa*, a miniature conifer and relative of the monkey puzzle tree. The Norfolk Island pine is an easy plant to grow indoors, having no particular requirements for warmth, light or humidity.

Dizygotheca elegantissima, sometimes known as the false aralia, is much more difficult to sustain. Tall, slim and elegant, with stems standing out from a single main trunk, and each bearing a compound leaf composed of eight to ten narrow, toothed segments, it likes a moderately warm atmosphere, tolerates a few hours of sun in winter (about 68°F, 20°C) but requires protection from all drafts. It is almost impossible to prevent the lower leaves from gradually falling to leave a bare stem at the base, but this can be disguised by setting it among other plants at floor level. On the other hand, this naked stem makes the plant appear more tree-like, which can, of course, be a desirable attribute in some indoor gardens.

Schefflera (Brassaia) actinophylla is a little tree with palmate green leaves growing at the end of reaching stems or stalks. It grows well and, making a large plant, is much in demand by decorators for floor tubs in houses and offices. It is sometimes known as the umbrella tree, although it is not nearly so like an umbrella as *Heptapleurum venulosa*, which is itself sometimes called *Schefflera*. The foliage here is smaller, more arching, and not unlike the ribs of an umbrella. It too will grow into a fairly large specimen in time.

It is a rare thing in the world of botany to find a bigeneric cross, a plant derived from two separate genera. But in *Fatshedera lizei*, which is a cross between a *Fatsia*, a shrub, and a *Hedera* or ivy, we have a first-class example. The fatshedera can be either a climber or tree-like, depending on how you treat it. It is generally sold as a specimen tree, its one or more main stems clipped or tied to a central stake. If this stake is extended from time to time, the plant can be induced to grow up into a tall, slim tree. An easy and accommodating plant, it has no particular preference for sun or shade, warm or cool conditions, or moist or dry soil.

Other indoor plants, including palms and bamboos, can be trained to grow tall, but most are hardly tree-like. And of the few genuinely tree-like plants mentioned here, all can be grown as shorter, rounder shrubs by the simple process of pinching out the main growing shoot or tip and allowing the side growth to develop. Some plants look quite attractive grown this way, largely because they differ from other varieties of the species.

Plant shapes

To a certain extent, the charm of all indoor plants depends on the way they fit into or highlight their immediate environment. So it is disappointing to bring home a plant, place it in a particular part of the home for which it is eminently suited and then to find after some months that it doesn't look quite right in its chosen spot. Since the plant is often quite healthy, the reason for its looking out of place is probably only that it has

Most indoor plants suffer from overwatering, but the graceful, tall and feathery *Cyperus alternifolius gracilis* is a bog plant and its roots can be allowed to paddle.

grown too large for its position, and this is a further reason to strictly limit the amount of food or fertilizer given to any plant. All plants must be kept growing if they are to be healthy and natural in appearance, but if they are overfed, they will grow large too quickly and often make abnormal leaf development. By thus outgrowing their strength, they will render themselves open to insects and diseases.

Too many indoor gardeners are so anxious that their plants should grow that they let them flourish quite untrained.

To take one example of this unwitting form of neglect we have only to look at the popular spider plant (*Chlorophytum comosum variegatum*), that easy, grass-like plant with slender arching green and cream leaves. This is usually brought home as a mere tuft some 6 in (15 cm) tall growing from the center of a small pot. It grows quickly and in only a few months will have developed into a central mass whence several arching

Ivies indoors can be trained to trail, climb, spread or become a tree or a bush. The picture on the right shows a climbing *Hedera canariensis*.

Many indoor plants grow differently in their natural surroundings. This bushy palm, *Neanthe bella* (1), would normally be a tall tree. *Pilea cadierei nana* (2) should have its growing tips pinched out regularly in order to keep it attractive and bushy. Tradescantias and zebrinas (3) are excellent trailers for the home if their stems are not allowed to grow too long. Philodendrons (4) vary widely, but many are climbers and some will cling with their roots to a nearby wall. The thick, fleshy, spear-like leaves of *Sansevieria trifasciata* (5) have given it the popular name of snake sansevieria.

stems bear a few tiny, white, and rather insignificant flowers. As each small flower becomes a miniature plantlet, a little tuft of leaves with rudimentary roots, the parent plant will drape itself over its original pot and cover the surface on which it stands. In a few more weeks it will cascade over shelf or table. If the plant happens to be standing on a tray filled with pebbles, peat moss or sand, each little plantlet will root in the medium, thereby compounding the problem. All this exuberant growth may look highly decorative for a time, but it will certainly be occupying more space than was originally envisaged.

If you want a big, blowsy, tumbling mass of green and cream leaves, then by all means leave it as it is, but give it enough space to look its best: do not confine its arching stems into little more than a dust trap. With enough space a healthy plant can look magnificent, but if there is not enough room and the plant is cramped and unhealthy, rescue the little plantlets at the end of the arching stems by resting them on a small pot of soil where they will quickly and easily take root. As soon as you have one or two small young plants growing well, move, discard or give away the parent plant and keep only the small plants, which will fit more comfortably and happily into the available space.

Several of the bromeliads will begin to die after they have flowered. This process may take several months or even years and in the meantime they will have produced a young plant from the soil in which they grow. It is quite possible to allow both plants to grow in the same pot until the elder plant has passed its prime, but it is

better to discard the old plant before this stage and to repot the new in fresh soil.

Some plants, particularly climbers, such as ivies, grape-ivy (*Cissus rhombifolia*) and kangaroo vine (*C. antarctica*), grow so exuberantly that in a year or so they will form a fat column of foliage from floor to ceiling or will cover a wall. Cutting away some of the long trails in order to thin the plant and make it more decorative again is possible but temporarily disfigures the plant. It is better to take a cutting or two and grow these to maturity, eventually discarding the old and overgrown plant. It is an easy matter to take such cuttings, for all that is needed is to take one of the trailers and remove several inches (centimeters) of foliage from one end. This bare stem should be buried in a pot of soil nearby until after a few weeks it is obvious from the new growth that it has taken root. It can then be separated from the parent plant.

On the other hand, it could be highly decorative to have a plant with a dozen or more trails up to 10 ft (3 m) long. They can easily be attached to a central pillar, cane or string, or can be trained to cover a wall surface by tying the trails to guide string or something similar. Ivy plants can be induced to cling to an undecorated indoor wall in much the same way as they would to a tree outside. Grape-ivy, kangaroo vine and the true ivies can all be trained into living curtains of greenery to divide any room. Lightly spraying a brick wall where the ivy grows will be sufficient to encourage the roots to take hold. It should be said, however, that these aerial roots are strong. They will do no real damage to the struc-

ture of the wall, but they will certainly mark wallpaper or other surfaces.

Certain climbers, such as ivies, some philodendrons, scindapsus and one or two others, can be encouraged to grow up special supports by tying a fat skin of sphagnum moss or some similar material around a central cane or stick, or alternatively by

Plant trailers can be made to cover a wall or form a partition. Fix the string or canes in position, then tie or clip each trailer.

stuffing a hollow cane of small mesh wire netting with the same material and attaching a trailer to it. The plant will quickly send up aerial roots into it, and will subsequently pull itself up with its own roots so long as the moss is kept moist.

Flowering plants

One of the main reasons why indoor plants make such excellent home decoration is that the majority depend for their effect on their foliage, which changes little over the seasons. Flowering plants are a different matter. They are, almost without exception, grown only for their flowers and when these have passed, the plant itself may have

Many plants will climb a cane covered with moist sphagnum moss, using their aerial roots. A cylinder of wire mesh stuffed with moss can be equally effective.

lost its interest and attraction. For this reason we classify some flowering plants as temporary decoration, to be used and enjoyed only while in flower. But there are some flowering plants, such as the many varieties of the dainty African violet, *Saintpaulia*, which can be kept flowering for almost the entire year; some like cineraria and calceolaria can be grown from seed; while a few, like the familiar and rightly popular *Impatiens walleriana*, or busy Lizzie (also known as patient Lucy and the patience plant), can be propagated from cuttings. There are herbaceous pot plants, such as chrysanthemums, which can be bought in flower or in bud, or can be raised from seed or from cuttings. And there are many, special plants, such as azaleas, cyclamens, poinsettias and the like, which are usually grown for special occasions and are only seldom retained for another year.

Bulbs are among the favorite indoor flowering plants. Apart from their obvious beauty and the fact that so many of them herald spring, a major reason for their

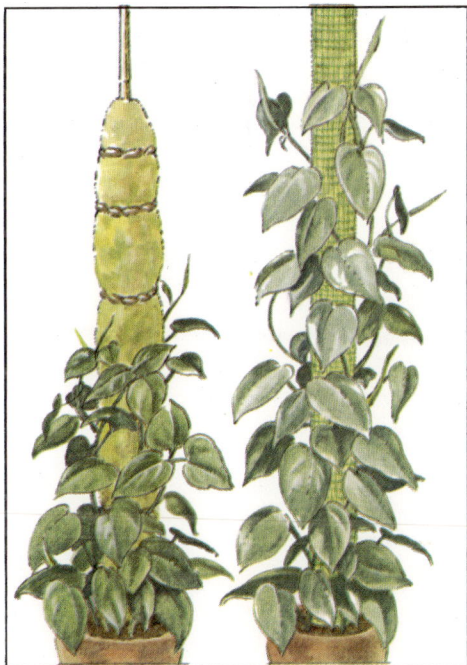

popularity is that one can follow their growth from their purchase as plain, brown-skinned spheres to their final flowering in the home.

Among the best spring-flowering bulbs to grow indoors are daffodils, tulips, hyacinths and crocuses. Some can be bought 'prepared', which means that they have been specially treated to flower early with less effort on the part of the indoor gardener.

The care of bulbs for indoor forcing can differ according to variety, so ask for instructions when you buy your bulbs. In general, indoor bulbs should be potted as soon as they are received or bought. Place 3–5 large bulbs, such as tulip or daffodil, in a 6 in (15 cm) pot, usually in late summer or early autumn. They should then be watered and placed outdoors in a trench about 12 in (30 cm) deep or in a cold shed, suitably protected from mice and other predators, until their roots have grown deep and strong and shoots are beginning to appear – usually in about six or more weeks. They can then be brought indoors into a cool atmosphere, watered as necessary and gradually introduced to normal living conditions, such as bright light, even direct sun, where they will soon come into flower.

Some plants are grown indoors for many years and they flower only occasionally, or sometimes never bloom at all. Cacti and epiphyllums are examples. Without knowing the specific conditions under which such plants are grown, dogmatic directions cannot be given. If the plants are strong and healthy and if they are mature enough to bloom, there is every probability that a change of treatment will in itself induce them to flower.

Special crocus pots show off the vivid flowers to best advantage.

Hyacinths grow well in bulb fiber.

Narcissus Cragford will thrive in pebbles.

Flowering plants must have good light (*see left*) to obtain good results.

One thing to bear in mind is that plants become accustomed to their surroundings and do not like to be moved from one position to another. Find a good spot for your plant and leave it there. If, on second thought, you think it should have more light or some other comfort, move it to what you think is a better place, but try not to shift plants around like furniture. You may find that flower buds tend to appear on a plant where the light is strongest, that is, on the window side of the plant. In this case encourage new buds by turning the pot a quarter turn a day so that all sides of the plant get a chance at the light.

One of the main reasons why a plant may refuse to flower is that it has been hurried along too much. All plants have a dormant, or resting, season and during this period

One needs to be a little more careful when buying an indoor flowering plant. Obviously, a plant that is smothered with bloom and vivid with color, will have the strongest appeal. But if it is at its peak, there is usually only one way it can go – downwards – one exception being the floriferous African violet. Look instead for a plant with a future, one with buds just beginning to open, with strong, green foliage and with the soil in the pot just moist. Never buy a plant with yellowing, drooping, limp or diseased foliage.

they should be given every assistance to rest by cutting down the amount of food and water they are given, perhaps even cutting down the amount of light they receive. At the other extreme, it must be kept in mind that some bloom-shy plants, certain begonias for instance, simply require more light to form buds.

In general, cacti and all other succulents will rest during the winter months and at this time their soil should be kept almost completely dry. If the atmosphere in the home is too warm and dry and some of the plants begin to suffer from extreme deprivation, a little more water will do no harm. But, on the whole, the plants will give a better performance in the summer months if they have been allowed to suspend their activities during the winter. When the warmer and longer days arrive, watering can be stepped up until in midsummer the plants may require as much water as non-succulents. They will swell and grow and, if the light is good, there is every chance that strange and beautiful flowers will appear on mature plants.

The one exception to this method of treating cacti in order to get them to flower is with the leaf, or epiphytic cacti. These include the popular Christmas cactus or *Schlumbergera truncata* (syn. *Zygocactus truncatus*), the Easter cactus *Rhipsalidopsis gaertneri*, the epiphyllums *Rhipsalis*, and the mistletoe cactus, all of which can produce such large, vivid and beautiful flowers that they have been called orchid cacti. In their native habitat these plants grow high on jungle trees instead of in rocky, desert soil,

If it is winter and the weather is cold or frosty, make sure that the plant is well wrapped when you bring it home. The wrapping paper should cover not only the pot, but the entire plant. At home, place the pot in a bucket of water, submerging it completely, unless the soil is very moist. Wait for the bubbles to rise and when these have ceased remove the pot and stand it to drain.

As the plant develops, the buds will gradually open into flowers, which will eventually fade. Cut them away once they have passed their best. Fading flowers give plants a shabby appearance, may let in disease and certainly consume available food and moisture in the soil without giving anything in return. Far better that this nourishment should go to the developing buds.

All flowering plants of whatever type need good light if they are to develop well, so stand your plant close to a window where it will not get direct sunlight for more than a few hours a day but where the light is usually good. Or grow it under fluorescent tubes for about 12–16 hours a day. Never stand it over a radiator or any other source of heat and, if possible, find a cool spot away from drafts.

Neoregelia carolinae tricolor, a bromeliad, turns a vivid scarlet at the center when its small blue and insignificant flowers appear in the characteristic cup, which should always be kept filled with water.

Zygocactus truncatus, the Christmas cactus, has several varieties and can have flowers of several colors. These appear at the tops of the long, flattened stems, which resemble leaves.

During the warmer months many indoor plants will enjoy periods outside in sun and rain.

Euphorbia milii (syn. E. splendens), the crown of thorns will flower continuously throughout its long life.

and for this reason require a different kind of treatment from other cacti.

The Christmas cactus flowers in midwinter, December in the northern hemisphere, June in the southern, so it will require good light and plenty of water at this time instead of being starved. Its resting period is in summer, when it can stand outdoors in partial shade and rain (not too much of this) to help the flat, leaf-like stems to ripen. Perhaps the easiest way to insure Christmas cactus flowers is to delay bringing the pots indoors after their summer sojourn outdoors. Since cool nights are needed to induce bud formation, leave the pots outdoors until fall is well advanced – mid-October in the northern hemisphere, mid-April in the southern – then bring the pots indoors to a cool, well-lighted window away from artificial light at night.

There are hundreds of varieties of epiphyllum, mainly in various shades of white, pink and red.

Some of our most colorful flowering house plants are known as traditional Christmas gifts. They include *Euphorbia pul-* *cherrima*, the poinsettia, the indoor cyclamen, *Cyclamen persicum*, otherwise *C. puniceum* or *C. latifolium*, and the rhododendron (*Azalea indica*). All do best under well-lighted, cool and airy conditions, hard to find in most apartments and many overheated dwellings. However, these plants show amazing stamina for survival if reasonable approximation of their needs is provided.

Poinsettia is grown mainly for its magnificent, red, pink or white bracts rather than its insignificant flowers, the berry-like objects at the top of the vivid bracts that many people mistakenly think are petals. As a result of a great deal of hybridizing, new varieties are now available that will last in the home for months instead of days. Such hybrids have been known to exist from Christmas to Christmas – the only change being a gradual fading of the bracts' color! They are bred under artificial conditions of daylight and darkness and with chemical treatment, which keeps them dwarf, bushy and well-colored. The roots of these plants should always be kept moist, but not wet, and a cool part of the room (about 60°F, 15°C) in good light will suit them best. It is possible to keep the plants after they have dropped their leaves and to

Epiphyllums (*above* and *below left*) have been the subject of much hybridization, as a result of which huge, magnificent and flamboyant flowers of many colors have been produced. Where space is limited, the plants can be pruned back.

bring them into condition for the following season, but this can be a tricky exercise best left to the expert. It is wise, though not essential, to prune away old stems after they have produced their flowers, because once a bloom has appeared at a particular spot no flower will ever be produced from there again. Try to encourage strong new growth each year to aid flower production since blooms appear on one and two-year-old branches. It is important to repot the plants if they grow too large for their containers.

Rhipsalis are like smaller, daintier versions of epiphyllums or orchid cacti and they require much the same kind of treatment. A light shade suits them better than strong sunlight and even in the winter their roots like a little water. Greater attention has been paid to rhipsalis in recent years, possibly because some of the epiphyllums grow too large.

A succulent that is not a cactus but a member of an extraordinarily wide-ranging family is the so-called crown of thorns, *Euphorbia milii*, which gets its name from the vicious black thorns growing from its stems and from its tiny vivid, red flowers, which look like drops of blood. Another form of the plant bears yellow flowers. This is an easy and striking plant to grow. It likes full sun and plenty of water most of the time and does not appear to need a resting period.

Cyclamens in full flower can be spectacularly beautiful but the conditions they meet in most homes are so unsuitable that they quickly lose their beauty. They like cool, fresh air and plenty of moisture. It is best not to grow them in living rooms unless you can place them in a bay window where the temperature is much lower than the rest of the room. They make excellent bedroom plants, where the temperature is

The cyclamen *(right)* is available in many colors. Cool conditions are necessary indoors for the plant to last and to continue producing its flowers.

The safest way to water a dry azalea plant *(above)* is to place the pot in a bucket of water, keeping the blooms dry. Wait until bubbles cease to rise from the soil surface, then drain and replace.

Modern varieties of poinsettia, *Euphorbia pulcherrima*, are long-lasting and easy to grow.

usually a little lower and the air fresher. Give them good light but they should never be placed in direct sun.

The rhododendron, or *Azalea indica*, has also been grown under highly artificial conditions for the Christmas trade. Its roots have usually been heavily pruned so that they will fit into a comparatively small pot, and this makes the plant highly sensitive to any shortage of water. The roots must be kept moist, but not soggy, at all times. The best indication of their state is the portion of brown main stem immediately above the soil. This should show up wet and dark for an inch or so. If it is a uniform light brown, the plant is badly in need of water. The best way to treat it is to plunge the entire pot into a bucket of tepid water, leaving it there until bubbles have ceased to rise from the soil surface. Then remove, drain and replace in position. The same cool indoor temperatures needed by the cyclamen apply also to the azalea, making it an ideal plant for a cool window, a plant room or a sun porch. Under such conditions the plants remain spectacular for many weeks. Potted plants can be summered outdoors in partial shade, sink the pots to their rims in soil, and leave outdoors until late fall before bringing the plants indoors for later bloom.

Because many flowering houseplants need 12-14 hours of sunlight each day, there are three methods you can use to obtain it.

1. Place your plants in a south window.

2. Install artificial lighting units that imitate natural sunlight. These units can be set up nearly anywhere in home or office.

3. Install a window greenhouse or erect a free-standing one. Each is available in a wide range of styles and sizes.

Below: azaleas, so often given as Christmas gifts, need special attention if they are to flower well. Their roots must always be kept moist for the plant to be at its best.

Exotics

One tends to think of exotic plants as orchids, yet some of these traditionally glamorous and difficult plants are comparatively easy to grow, while other and apparently less 'exotic' plants are much more difficult.

The many caladium hybrids, for example, have what is possibly the most beautiful foliage of any plant, at least 12 in (30 cm) long, so fine and thin as to be almost translucent, in pale greens and creams or more vivid tints and shades. The main veins are usually picked out in contrasting colors. These plants need to be kept warm, though not uncomfortably so (about 68°F, 20°C) and in conditions that are as humid as can conveniently be arranged, not so difficult to find on most summer terraces and patios. They grow from tubers, which come into leaf in spring, display their beautiful leaves until midsummer and then begin to fade. The tubers should then be put away in their pots in a place that is warm and dry, and completely forgotten until early spring, when they can be potted up in a peaty soil mixture and brought into a warm, moist atmosphere for the foliage to begin growing.

Smaller, thicker and more sturdy leaves appear on the dieffenbachias, and, although less ethereal and longer lasting, the foliage can also be very beautiful – streaked, spotted, blotched and marbled, usually in various tints of cream and green. *Dieffenbachia picta* and *D. amoena* both have leaves spotted and blotched with cream, and tolerate warmth and low-light levels typical of so many modern rooms. Two popular new hybrids are 'Exotica' and 'Rudolph Roehrs'. The second has large chartreuse leaves which are edged with dark green.

The dieffenbachias are collectively

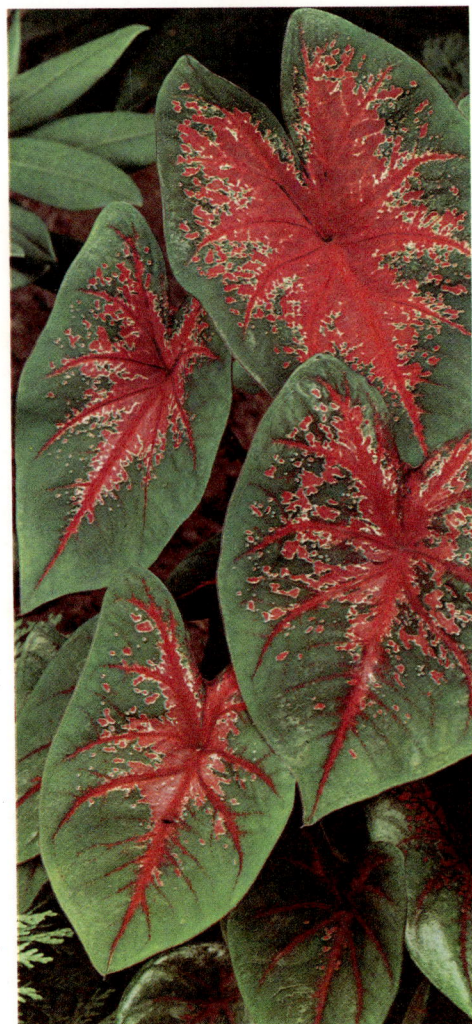

The dignified beauty of *Dieffenbachia amoena* (*above*) fits well into the clean lines of modern decor.

Caladium hybrids develop in spring and must be kept in a warm and humid atmosphere to give of their best.

22

Dieffenbachia leaves, which can grow to a considerable size, are strikingly marked. Keep them warm, out of drafts in moist soil.

Philodendron oxycardium will cling to a wall or a mossed cane with its aerial roots.

If kept out of full sun and intense heat, caladiums should remain attractive until mid to late summer.

known as dumb canes, the reason being that their sap contains crystals of calcium oxalate, which causes the tongue to swell painfully if they are taken into the mouth. Plants can be handled perfectly safely – it is only the sap that is poisonous. So if a fading leaf is cut away, for example, it is wise to take precautions and wash the hands thoroughly after the operation.

Most members of the large and useful philodendron clan, mentioned earlier, are easy to grow and quite dependable as well as being comparatively ordinary. *P. melanochrysum* has the same heart-shaped leaves as *P. oxycardium* (syn. *P. scandens* and *P. cordata*), the well-known heartleaf philodendron or sweetheart vine. But although they are about the same shape and size, their color and texture are completely different, the former being a rich green-bronze-gold-copper and having a velvety texture on the upper surface. High humidity, warm temperatures, rich soils and no drafts are demanded by this plant.

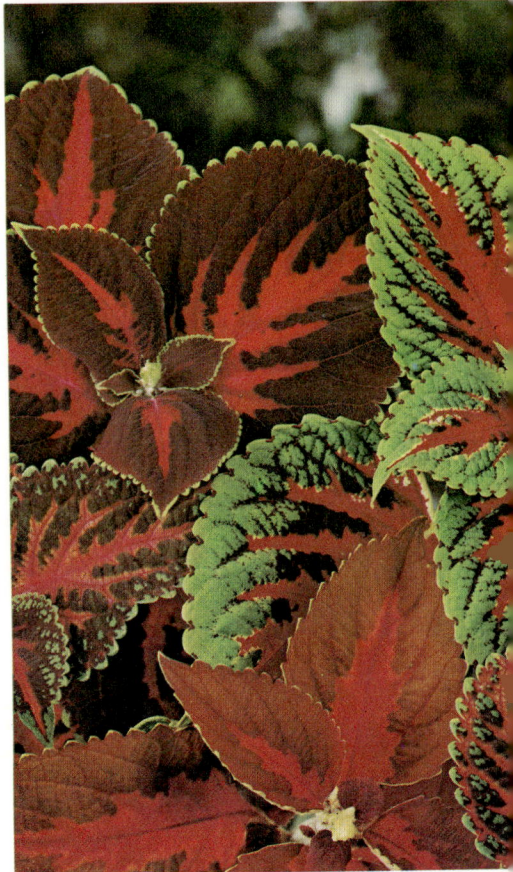

Begonia masoniana, popularly known, for obvious reasons, as the iron cross begonia, is named after Maurice Mason, an English farmer and distinguished plantsman. Its crinkled, patterned and hairy leaves make it instantly recognizable.

Coleus plants in the widest variations of vivid colors are easy to grow from seed or cuttings. They grow indoors and, in warm areas, in the garden. They like moist soil and plenty of food.

Several of the foliage begonias could be called exotics because of the extraordinary and vivid colors or textures of their leaves. *Begonia rex*, the ivy-leafed begonia, and *B. masoniana* are examples that come immediately to mind. Both will bear flowers but these are insignificant compared to the leaves, which in the former can vary widely in tints, shades, tones and patterns of greens and reds, purples, silvers and whites, some almost furry and others metallic. *B. masoniana* is known as the iron cross begonia because of the distinctive pattern on the soft and crinkled leaves. All begonias, flowering or foliaged, have the same lopsided heart shape in their leaves. Some people find them difficult to cultivate, others easy, and arguments continue about their care. A rich, peaty soil, some warmth, some light (all begonias do especially well under artificial light) and no particular concessions to humidity seem to summarize the general view. Taking care not to overwater begonias can go far towards avoiding trouble.

Two other beautiful plants with vividly colored foliage are *Codiaeum variegatum*, usually called croton, and *Coleus blumei*. The first has handsome spotted, streaked and mottled leaves, is glossy surfaced and comes in several shapes. The colors are green, gold, cream, red, pink, purple and white. Unless you have a warm plant room, window area or a combination greenhouse-living room where the humidity can be depended on to be high and the light ample – even several hours of sun each day – you had better pass crotons by, as they are not the easiest of plants to grow in the home. Coleus plants can be just as colorful as crotons but, unlike them, their texture is soft and sappy. These plants can be grown quite easily from seed or cuttings.

Three other plants with gorgeous foliage are the prayer plants, maranta, the calatheas and the fittonias. The most distinctive maranta is *M. leuconeura erythroneura*, which has soft leaves of brownish green, with the veins picked out in scarlet edged with cream. Even better known is *M. l. kerchoveana*, sometimes called 'rabbits' tracks' because of the brown-on-green marking of the leaves.

Calathea mackoyana is sometimes known as *Maranta mackoyana*, which it closely resembles. It is commonly known as the peacock plant because of the sheer flamboyance of its leaf coloration and pattern. The colors are silver, green, red, or purple, according to the way the light strikes it, for the upper and lower sides of the leaves differ and the white part is almost translucent except for the dark green veins. Humidity, careful watering so the soil remains moist, and some warmth and diffused light are needed to keep this plant looking its best. It is a good subject for growing under artificial light, but its greatest need is for high humidity.

And finally in this little trio is the snake-skin, or nerve plant, *Fittonia vershaffeltii argyroneura,* small, delicate and beautifully patterned, as the common name suggests. Too much water will kill the plant, as will too little. Cold will kill it and so will excessive heat. A plant in bright sun will curl up and die almost as you watch it. Somewhat easier to grow is *F. verschaffeltii*, with rather larger leaves, a more velvety texture and a basic green color with red veins.

It is worth persevering with all these difficult and delicate plants, for the sensitive and persistent plant-grower will eventually discover the exact conditions or treatment a certain plant requires.

The peacock plant, *Calathea mackoyana*, is often called *Maranta mackoyana*. With reasonable care this plant will keep its looks for long periods.

So too with orchids, which are as easily grown in the house as a hyacinth. Begin with the simplest and progress to the more difficult, not a hard thing to do when one realizes that there must be something like 25,000 orchid species in the world, that something like ten per cent of all flowering plants in the world are orchids, that they grow wild in jungles, mountains, woodlands, meadows and on roadside verges in many of our most industrialized nations. Orchids were treated with awe when the only examples we saw were those in museums or in the orchid houses of the rich. Those days are over. Many kinds of orchids have been found to be as tolerant of ordinary indoor conditions as common house plants. Although they thrive in window

gardens, they also respond well to artificial light. New methods of propagation mean that a thousand young plants can be easily and inexpensively produced where only a single plant existed before.

All orchids have three petals and three sepals, but one of these petals is usually grown in another form, looking more like a pouch or slipper, and is frequently differently colored or patterned. Just above this curiously shaped petal, known sometimes as the labellum or lip, is the column. This single organ takes the place of the more usual male and female stamen and pistil.

Probably the best known of the slipper orchids are the species commonly called cypripediums, although botanically they are correctly *Paphiopedilum. P. insigne* is one of the easier to grow as well as one of the most popular. From 3–6 in (7–15 cm) long, they are generally a greenish-gold with brownish spots and they last from three to eight weeks during their winter season. A great deal of breeding work has been done on the paphiopedilums and there are a large number of hybrids. One of the best known is probably *P. x. Maudial* with beautiful marbled leaf rosettes and long-lasting green and white flowers.

There are a considerable number of paphiopedilums. Some are comparatively large, both as plants and as flowers, while others are less than 4 in (10 cm) tall. Most species have only a single flower to a stem, but some have two, three or four.

The paphiopedilums do not require high temperatures – the cooler the temperature, the longer the flowers last – or strong light, which is one reason why they grow well indoors. But, needless to say, they like as much humidity as they can get, and their compost or potting medium should always be kept moist, although not soggy. All orchid nurseries will sell special orchid compost, usually made of a mixture of osmunda fiber, sphagnum or peat moss, perlite and perhaps some granular peat.

Only one or two of the paphiopedilums have any fragrance, but many of the cattleyas are scented. Instead of a slipper or pouch, cattleyas have a more open, bell-shaped lip, frequently prettily frilled and divided. The cattleyas come in two types, the labiate, or unifoliate, with only one leaf growing from each pseudo-bulb, and the bifoliates with two leaves. There are many hybrids in each type, some large, some dwarf, some with flowers up to 10 in (25 cm) wide, and others with blooms no larger than 2 in (5 cm). Cattleyas like a fairly warm and humid atmosphere and need a drop in temperature at night.

Most cattleyas grow to nearly 3 ft (about 1 m) in height, too large for some homes, but there are some miniature cattleyas offered by specialists. Cymbidiums will grow to nearly 6 ft (over 2 m). However, there is a useful and attractive group of hybrid dwarf cymbidiums, which grow about 12 in (30 cm) or so tall. The color range of the very long-lasting flowers is magnificent. Cymbidiums require a growing compost of fir bark, coarse peat moss and bark fiber, adequate humidity and good light. Keep the compost moist, but not soggy. One of the easiest groups to grow indoors is the odontoglossum, with many species and even more hybrids. It is also one of the most rewarding because of the number of flowers per stem – from about 5 to 35 – and the colors – whites, yellows, reds, pinks, purples. The flowers, which appear in the spring, will last from 3 to 6 weeks. Plants dislike too much heat in both winter and summer, and prefer to be well ventilated, although never in a draft. The roots should be kept moist at all times.

Also considered rewarding for beginners are the laelias; small, epithytic and with cattleya-shaped flowers, varying from 2 to 20 per stem.

Two little orchids that more often are available from bulb specialists rather than the usual orchid sources are *Pleione formosana* and *Bletilla* (syn. *Bletia*) *striata*. Although they are considered fairly hardy, enduring temperatures to 40°F (4°C), and therefore can be planted in the open in semi-shade and a humus-rich soil, they are also grown in pots. Pleione bears small magenta-pink flowers in spring. Bletilla is similar, but the lavender-pink flowers appear in early summer. Advertised as easy to cultivate by the mail-order firms that sell these semi-hardy orchids from Asia, they may in fact prove difficult to grow outdoors.

Opposite: this small selection of orchids gives some indication of the wide variation in shape and color available. Light is their most important requirement, then humidity and warmth. Feed only in summer and keep out of drafts.

Paphiopedilums (*right*) must have humidity and a moist soil, but need less warmth.

The dainty orchid flowers of *Bletilla striata* (*below*) are easy to obtain indoors in early summer.

Food for thought

There is a curious fascination in growing a plant left over from one's food. To plant an orange 'pip' or seed and watch the little tree growing a few weeks later is always satisfying, and there are several plants that can be grown in this way. Not all will live for long indoors, although the avocado and mango are examples of two exceptionally attractive and durable house plants that can be grown from 'left-overs'.

The miniature orange trees that one can

buy, complete with little oranges, are no more than an acknowledgement of the fascination of growing a plant from a seed that was saved from the garbage can. Do not expect to produce oranges bursting with juicy goodness from your own home-grown tree, however. The flower- and fruit-covered plant you buy is a special dwarf kind, the calamondin orange (*Citrus mitis*). The white flowers are sweetly scented and they appear on the little tree at the same time as the fruits, which are reputed to make a good marmalade.

Keep the plant in a cool place that is sunny or, at least, well-lit. Keep it well fed and slightly humid. Flowers of *Citrus mitis* produce more fruits if they are fertilized, so when they are fully open it is wise to brush them all very gently with a very soft camel-hair brush.

An avocado seed – so large it resembles a stone – is easy to grow either in soil or water. Plant it only halfway into the soil and watch it split in two as the shoot begins to appear. Or grow it in a hyacinth glass or a jar, its blunt base just touching the water and the more pointed end upwards. (Three toothpicks inserted into the sides of the seed are handy for suspending the seed on the rim of the jars.) Sometimes you will get a single shoot that grows very quickly and quite tall before it puts out its first leaf. In this case, pinch out the growing tip after it has produced several leaves to induce the plant to bush out more attractively.

Mustard and cress, mung beans, alfalfa,

sesame, wheat and several other sprouting foods can be grown easily enough indoors.

Mustard and cress, so good in winter salads, are easily and quickly grown in a small seedling box or flat on a kitchen windowsill. Fill the tub with any of the prepared mixes available from garden centers and florists or use your own general-purpose soil mixture. Soak well, then sow seeds thickly, merely pressing them into the mixture rather than covering. Slip the flats into a polyethylene kitchen bag and keep from direct sun until the seeds germinate. Remove the bag and place flats in bright light on a windowsill or under fluorescent lights. Cut the seedlings with scissors after a few weeks. Successively sow and crop for a constant supply. Seeds of the other crops, available from most mail-order seed houses usually require different treatment. The easiest way to grow seeds is to put a spoonful into a clear glass jar and cover the neck tightly with muslin or cheesecloth. Pour in a little tepid water through the muslin, shake the seeds around in this, leave for a few minutes and then stand the jar on its side so the water runs out again. Repeat this process for three or four days until it is evident that the seeds have begun to grow.

Plant grown from an avocado seed.

The easiest way to grow seeds is to put a spoonful of them into a clear glass jam (or other) jar and then cover the neck tightly with muslin.

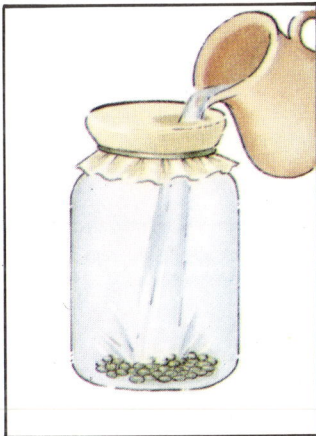

Pour in a little tepid water through the muslin, shake the seeds around, leave for a few minutes, then stand the jar on its side so the water runs out again.

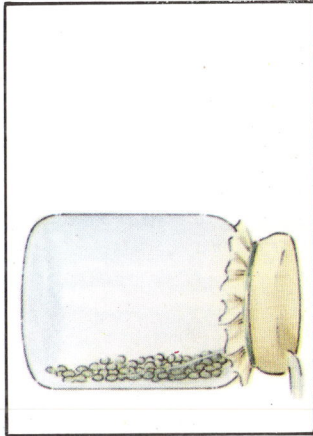

Repeat this process for three or four days. It then will be evident that the seeds have begun to grow. Remove them when they are large enough to eat.

A variety of herbs can be pot-grown outdoors and brought in as needed. This bouquet (*bottom left*) includes parsley, marjoram, dill, coriander, borage and tarragon.

Chives (*above left*) or tarragon (*above right*) are among the herbs which can be forced into early growth indoors.

Pots of parsley can be grown on a kitchen windowsill.

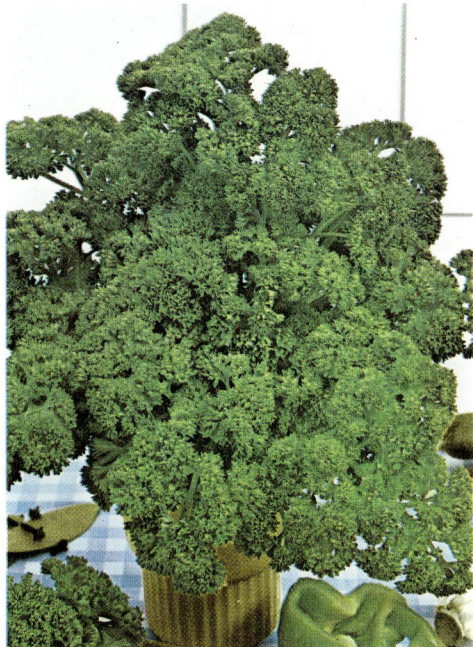

Care of house plants

A selection of the most popular house plants is given below. From this you can tell at a glance what watering, light, temperature and atmospheric moisture conditions your plants need for healthy growth. However, iron cross begonias, cyclamens and poinsettias need different conditions during their dormant periods. Consult your florist about this when you buy the plants.

Legend			
Watering	heavy	moderate	light
Light	sunny	semi-shady	shady
Temperature	warm	average	cool
Atmosphere	very moist	moist	average
Care needed	much	average	little
Flowering season	winter	spring · summer	autumn

Plant	Watering	Light	Temperature	Atmosphere	Care needed	Flowering season
Azalea	heavy	semi-shady	cool	moist	much	spring
Begonia masoniana (iron cross begonia)	heavy	semi-shady	cool	moist	much	—
Cacti	light	sunny	cool	average	little	winter / spring / summer
Chlorophytum (spider comosum plant)	heavy	semi-shady	cool	moist	little	—
Chrysanthemums	heavy	sunny	cool	moist	much	spring / summer
Cissus antarctica (kangaroo vine)	heavy	semi-shady	cool	moist	little	—
Coleus blumei	heavy	semi-shady	cool	moist	little	—
Cyclamen persicum	heavy	semi-shady	cool	very moist	much	spring
Euphorbia pulcherrima (poinsettia)	heavy	semi-shady	cool	moist	much	—
Epiphyllum	light	semi-shady	cool	moist	little	(autumn)
Ficus elastica (rubber tree)	light	semi-shady	cool	moist	much	—
Hedera helix (English ivy)	heavy	semi-shady	cool	moist	little	—
Monstera deliciosa (Swiss cheese plant)	heavy	shady	average	moist	much	—
Philodendron scandens (sweetheart plant)	heavy	shady	cool	moist	much	—
Saintpaulia (African violet)	heavy	semi-shady	cool	moist	much	winter / spring / summer
Sansevieria trifasciata (snake plant)	light	semi-shady	cool	moist	little	—
Tradescantia (wandering jew)	heavy	semi-shady	cool	moist	little	—

2 Environment

Light

The simple statement that giving a plant light is more important than giving it water will come as a surprise to most indoor gardeners until they begin to examine the proposition in greater depth. In the first place, to deprive a plant of light is a total deprivation. It carries no sources of light within itself. But to deprive a plant of water is less important because the soil in which it is growing is almost certainly moderately moist, and every root, branch, stem and leaf also contains moisture.

As humans we can recognize the importance of moisture much more easily than we can recognize the importance of light. We can tell if a plant has been watered by the color of the surface soil, by the feel of it on our fingers and by the weight of the pot. But we would find it difficult to measure the difference in the quality of light at a south-facing window and in the center of a room. Only by using the mechanical aid of a photo-electric light meter can we recognize the vast difference, a difference of minor importance to us but vital to plants. After all, the reason why plants are grown in greenhouses is to give them not only warmth or protection, but also the maximum possible light.

The quantity of light a plant receives will depend upon the length of day and hence the season, unless one wishes to go into the question of artificial light. Actually, the quantity of light is more important than is generally realized, for some plants such as chrysanthemums are short-day plants, which is to say that they will flower only when they receive a certain limited amount of daylight. This can be critical, and commercial growers have learned to extend the season by growing chrysanthemums for a period each day under the artificial but total shade of black plastic sheets. Other plants, conversely, are grown under artificial light to lengthen their day and so bring on their flowering.

In the home we unquestioningly accept the seasons as they come and we are more concerned about the quality than the quantity of the light our plants receive. This quality of light can vary surprisingly. Light in an industrial city, for example, is considerably weaker than light in the cleaner air of the countryside. Light in a room with a tree immediately outside is much less than in one without, but if the tree is not an evergreen, we can expect more light in the winter when it drops its foliage. Light from a south-facing window is stronger than from a window facing north. Light from a grimy window can equal that from a clean one half its size. Above all, light loses its intensity or quality in inverse proportion to the square of the distance from its source.

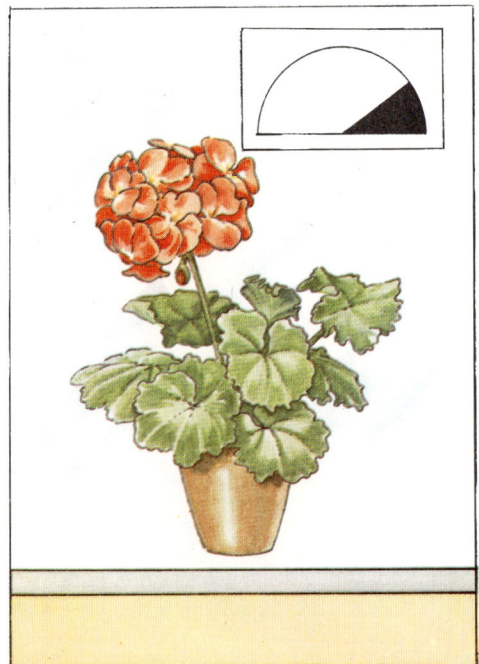

Light is vital to plants. Those that flower or have variegated foliage need most light, though not direct sunlight.

Never allow any plants to spend a wintry night between curtain and windowpane, where they can easily become frosted.

Cacti and some other succulents are the only plants that can tolerate direct sun on them for long periods of time.

This means, then, that in general terms plants should be placed as near to the windows as possible. But this advice must be qualified in some ways. Only cacti and some other succulents can be grown directly in a south-facing window in summer. In other seasons most house plants, with the exception of some large-leaved foliage plants, thrive in sunny windows. If the sunshine seems too strong – some signs of this are yellow or brown-tipped leaves – move the plants back or diffuse the light with curtains. No plants should ever be placed directly in a window that is loose, cracked, or allows drafts to pierce through. Nor should plants be placed between a window and a curtain during times of frost.

It is possible to divide our plant residents into groups: those that demand the most

Plants with dark green, fleshy leaves can generally tolerate poorly lit locations better than can plants which are brighter.

light, those that need good light, those that like a steady and modest light, and, finally, those that will grow farther away from light. In the same order, choose a south window, an east or west window, a north window and the center of a room or a position away from the light. Follow these rules: all cacti and succulents in strong light, even sunlight; all flowering plants and those with variegated foliage in good light, including several hours of sun; all others in

Top left: plants with variegated foliage tend to lose their attractive coloring if they do not get a regular quota of good light.

the less favored positions. Remember that the darker green and fleshier the leaf, the less light a plant usually needs.

Yet the possibility must be faced that many homes and apartments are woefully lacking in the wide range of natural light, described above, as well as sufficient window space for a number of plants. The solu-

Top right: try to place plants in positions where they will each receive the amount of light they need. They will look better and grow better as a result.

Cacti and succulents react favorably both to strong light and to warmth. Give plenty of water in summer but keep their roots almost dry in colder months.

tion is artificial light and its utilization to supplement natural light is one of the major factors in the current boom in indoor gardening. The set-up can be as extensive or as limited as one chooses. Entire basements or sections therein or other dim-lighted rooms have been transformed into greenhouses and plant rooms, the only source of light for plant growth coming from artificial sources. However, far less complicated arrangements are usual, ranging from simple table model fixtures that can accommodate a surprising number of African violets beneath them to fluorescent tubes installed under a bookcase shelf or a kitchen shelf and even to large, hanging fixtures suspended from the ceiling and raised or lowered as necessary according to the plants' heights.

Beginners often ask why fluorescent rather than incandescent light is specified for plant growth. Actually, incandescent light does benefit plants – and at the same time creates a more pleasing, less glaring illumination for us. A reading lamp that is turned on every evening will improve the growth of the plant beneath it. However, incandescent bulbs give off heat, enough to burn the plants that are too close to them, and are not as economical as the longer-lasting fluorescents, which also are capable of lighting broader areas. The market is now flooded with various kinds of fluorescent tubes and incandescent bulbs engineered to give plants the next best illumination to sunshine. There are several excellent books on the subject. For the time being, however, it is sufficient to point out to the reader that every plant discussed in this book will respond to artificial light.

Too often plants given as gifts are displayed in the living-rooms of homes where the air is polluted with tobacco fumes. (Orchids, in particular, hate smoke.)

The buds of cyclamen will develop and open and the flowers will remain fresh-looking for long periods if the plants are kept in a well-lit but cool and airy location.

35

If a plant must be placed over a source of heat, protect it by standing in a tray filled with gravel or sand kept just moist. The warmth will cause the water to evaporate and keep the plant cool.

Warmth

A certain amount of warmth is necessary for nearly all indoor plants, but less than is generally believed. All ivies, for example, are quite hardy and in most temperate climates will grow as well in the garden as in the house, although possibly with a change in characteristics. Many plants such as cyclamen will remain fresh and immaculate weeks longer in a cool room with a temperature of about 50°F (10°C) than in one heated to the more normal 70°F (20°C).

There is a common fallacy that indoor plants are hot-house plants, but this is not so. Some, it is true, have been bred from plants that originally grew in overheated and humid greenhouses, but without exception these have been educated to accept more realistic living conditions. So long as the home is heated sufficiently to keep out frosts, many indoor plants will grow there quite happily. They will prefer slightly higher temperatures, but given a choice between cooler conditions with clean air and some humidity, and warmer conditions with a stuffy atmosphere and dry air, they will do better in the former.

Most indoor plants, especially those that rely for their interest and attraction on their foliage, have their resting period in the colder months. They remain semi-dormant for some weeks. Their watering should be cut down during this period and they should be fed hardly at all. Yet if they are in too warm an atmosphere, the moisture in the soil around their roots will be baked away and the plants will either wilt or require more water. This will tend to activate the plants into renewed growth before their rest period has been completed.

No plant should be placed too near a source of heat, whatever its type. Even the sun can be too hot for some plants at some times of the day, particularly if it shines through glass. Incandescent bulbs can scorch plants that are closer to them than 12 in (30 cm). If for some special reason a plant must be placed, say, over a radiator,

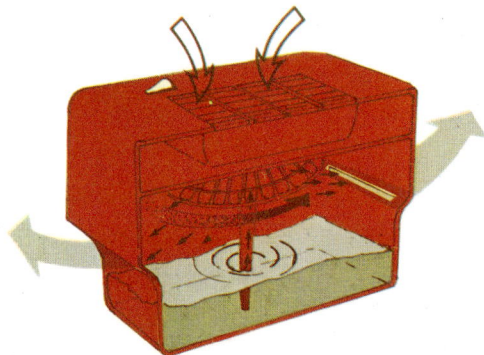

Humidity

We have become accustomed to associating humidity with high temperatures, which need not be so. For example, in a centrally heated room in winter with the temperature at, say, 70°F (20°C) we will find that the relative humidity reading on a hygrometer may fall to 50° or perhaps even less. With a window or two open, the temperature drops but the relative humidity rises. This is simply because the moisture in the room has been evaporated by the heat, and when the windows were closed, the outer air with its inherent moisture could not enter.

When we consider that all plants either grow or originally grew out–of–doors, it

then it is usually possible to deflect the rising warm air from the leaves of the plant. Another means of providing some protection is to stand the plant on a gravel tray filled with water. The rising hot air will, by this means, produce a moist atmosphere and so do little harm.

Try to avoid great differences of temperature at different times. Some rooms, for example, are heated only in the evenings; during the night they cool off and in the mornings they can be quite cold. Most plants dislike violent changes, although they will adapt to gradual ones. There are, however, a few plants, such as some orchids, that definitely need a temperature drop of several degrees at night to conform with the cooler nights of their tropical habitat.

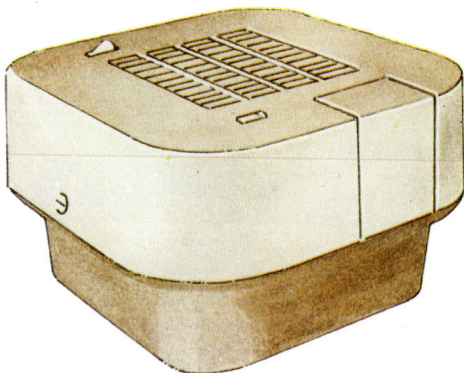

The most efficient humidifiers send a gentle current of moist air into the room from a reservoir of warmed water (*top left*). One type is shown above.

A significant rise in relative humidity can be gained by placing small bowls of water about the house. They can be made to look decorative with flowers, shells or stones.

Using a plunge pot lessens the risk of overwatering, keeps the flower pot cool and moist, and sends a constant current of humid air up around the plant foliage.

of one or two saucers or dishes of water in a room can significantly raise the humidity level. It is possible to buy quite inexpensive metal containers designed to hang on the back of a radiator that, when filled, gradually increase humidity by releasing water vapor into the room.

Plants can be given their own local humidity without much trouble by standing their pots on a tray holding a layer of constantly moist gravel pebbles or sand, or by making use of what English gardeners call 'plunge pots.'

This last aid is important for several reasons. The vast majority of indoor plants are grown in the traditional pot, either clay or plastic, with a hole or several holes in the base for drainage. This means that indoors the pot must be stood in a saucer or some other receptacle to avoid staining or marking the furniture. It is very easy when a plant is watered for the water to come through the drainage hole, fill the saucer and spill onto the furniture. Or we may find that the saucer is filled with water and, unknown to its owner, the plant may be drowning for several days.

The plunge pot is a means of overcoming the problem of providing a localized humidity and of increasing the decorative value of the plant all at the same time. This is a container of some kind that has no drainage hole and is a little larger than the flower pot. It can be a purpose-made pot, a flower vase, a bucket, a salad bowl, almost anything that is decorative. It should be selected for its suitability and its appearance so that it blends or contrasts with the plant color, texture, size and shape. This container should have a good layer of peat moss or some other moisture-retentive material placed at the base and the flower pot should be stood on this, while the space between the pot and its cover should also be filled with peat moss.

Now when the plant is watered any excess will be absorbed by the peat moss without doing any damage. The peat moss will also serve to insulate the flower pot

should be apparent that they will require a greater degree of humidity than is generally found in our houses. In most areas of the temperate world relative humidities out-of-doors probably range between about 60° and 80°. The first figure is sufficient for most of our plants indoors, but is a higher figure than is generally found indoors.

So if humidity is low we should do something about it; fortunately this is a simple matter. There is a large range of humidifiers on the market, from complex and expensive electric machines to the simplest, which are virtually no more than a pan of water and a fan. Even the provision from extremes of temperature. The peat moss will gradually release its moisture to the air and waft a slightly humid breeze upwards around the leaves of the plant.

Nearly all plants enjoy an occasional bath such as they might get during a summer shower, and when conditions allow, it is a good thing to put most plants out into a light rain for an hour or two, allowing them to drain and dry out before they are replaced in position. Many plants in the home can be given their own artificial rain occasionally with a spray of clean tepid water while others can luxuriate in a sink or shower. Such a bath should not be given to flowering plants or those with furry foliage.

There is one plant with furry foliage that benefits greatly by an occasional humidity bath and this is the beautiful and tender saintpaulia, or African violet. One way of helping it is to give it a steam bath. Make a little island of, say, an upturned saucer, in the center of a larger receptacle. Stand the saintpaulia on this in a waterproof container. Pour boiling water into the bowl, which should fall just short of the level of the pot. The issuing steam will benefit the plant. Leave it there until the water has become cool.

Pressure sprayers such as these produce a film of moisture which is so fine that there is no risk of damage to furnishings.

A steam bath takes time and trouble but is a great help to sensitive plants such as African violets when the atmosphere is too hot and dry. Many other types of plant will benefit from this treatment too.

3 Decorative uses

As furnishings

Nothing decorates a room more quickly than a few indoor plants. They soften sharp corners, drape bare walls, fill empty space and give personality to a previously anonymous area. A young couple setting up house for the first time can temporarily fill their empty spaces with plants instead of furniture, and even when they have acquired carpets, tables and chairs the plants will still be useful and decorative adjuncts to their home.

For the more established dwelling, plants can be employed for theatrical effect. You can hide a stained wall or disguise an unpleasant view from a window by suspending a row of plants that act as a 'curtain'.

You can even change the apparent shape

A wide spreading trailer will make a room appear wider than it is.

A climbing monstera will take the eye up to its tip and make a room appear higher than it really is.

or size of a room to a certain degree by using your plants as room dividers. Open shelf constructions are ideal places to display plants. Or simply use several tall, tubbed plants as 'living' walls.

If you want to make a low-ceilinged room look taller, select one or two tall tree-like plants, such as bamboo, podocarpus or schefflera palm, to create the illusion.

Indoor plants can be used most effec-

tively as dividers for rooms, separating the dining area from the cooking area, for example. These room dividers can be formed of shelves, or even small and specially made trolleys which are filled with plants. Take care, however, to ensure that when watering the plants no excess water falls on to furnishings. Also, the divider should be rigid enough to withstand the activities of young children, who might spill soil and plants onto the carpets. It may be necessary to move the plants from one place to another, to give them equal exposure to light.

Climbers

Tree ivies, grape-ivy and kangaroo vine, heartleaf philodendron, hoya, the black-eyed Susan vine (*Thunbergia alata*) and German ivy (*Senecio macroglossus variegatus* and *S. mikanioides*) are all easy and popular climbers that can be used to great decorative advantage in the home. Train them to climb a pole, to outline a window, to act as a soft green frame to a doorway or interior arch. Most can be tied or clipped to a cane, or even to heavy string fixed from floor to ceiling, which is easily hidden.

A screen of plants need not be dense and overpowering. A single plant such as a cissus can be woven through canes to look almost like a hedge or, as here, several different plants can play a more decorative role.

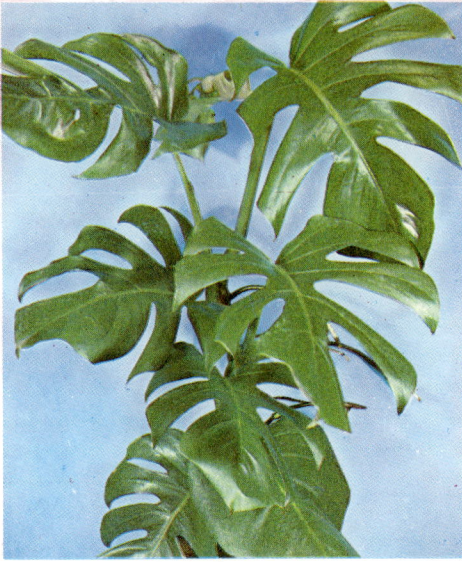

A climbing plant suited to the larger home or to office or showrooms is the fascinating *Monstera deliciosa*, known popularly as the Swiss cheese plant because of the holes, perforations and slashes in the large leaves. This will grow up a wall and grow right around the room if allowed to, a decorative characteristic which can be most useful. This, and certain other plants, present a problem because of the production of aerial roots – long, thong-like shoots that appear on branches and trail downwards. In their native state these aerial roots serve a useful purpose in drawing sustenance from the soil to higher portions of the plant, but in the home they are sometimes apt to be an embarrassment, for they are not particularly attractive. It is obvious that, in theory, the best thing to do with

Cissus antarctica, or kangaroo vine, a natural climber, is easy to cultivate and quick to respond to care. It is best grown up a string or a cane support.

these aerial roots is to lead them down into the original container of soil, or if this is too far away, into a secondary or subsidiary pot, for this way they will help to feed and encourage plant growth. On the other hand, if you have no objection to the plant growing perhaps a little less speedily, lushly and large, then there is no reason why these roots should not be cut neatly from the plant and thrown away.

Opposite: *Monstera deliciosa*, the Swiss cheese plant, will grow very large, so for limited spaces it is better to choose the smaller *M. pertusa* or *M.d. borsigiana*.
Below left: the popular *Hedera helix* 'Chicago'
Below right: the so-called German ivy, *Senecio macroglossus variegatus*.

Trailers

All climbers can, of course, also be trailers. In fact the vogue for hanging baskets has shown that there is no limit to the kinds of plants suitable for this purpose, whether as inhabitants of hanging baskets or whether tumbling from a bracket or shelf. Ordinary non-trailing house plants suspended in space, with their containers supported by macrame rope or cord hangers, assume a different character and dimension. A few of the non-trailing plants that are handsome in hanging baskets are African violets, most kind of begonias, especially those with colored foliage, piggyback plant (*Tolmiea men-*

43

Contrast in shape, size and texture. The monstera on the floor reaches up to the plectranthus growing above and tumbling downwards. Both are easy to grow.

ziesii) and many cacti and succulents. Yet these and the usual trailers need careful grooming to look their best. Plants in hanging containers, especially when in wire baskets filled with sphagnum moss, can dry out quickly in overheated rooms.

Among the more useful trailers are strawberry-begonia (*Saxifraga sarmentosa*), *Peperomia orba*, known as 'Princess Astrid' peperomia, and *P. glabella*, and the delightful easy, eager and decorative *Plectranthus purpuratus*, purple-leaved Swedish ivy. The last is prolific. It has almost round leaves 1–2 in (3–5 cm) across, dark green with a purple fuzz. It produces clouds of dainty lilac flowers through the summer. There are several other Swedish ivy varieties that are equally attractive as trailers.

A first-class, easy and strikingly attractive fern that grows well as a trailer is the elkhorn fern, *Platycerium alcicorne*. This grows dramatic fronds or leaves similar to a stag's horns, glaucous blue and slightly furry, from a central ball. The plant can be knocked from its pot and nailed or tied to a

This little trailing fig, *Ficus pumila*, needs moist and humid conditions to give of its best. It grows well twining among other plants in a mixed bowl.

Philodendron oxycar dium, the sweetheart plant, has better foliage and will cling to walls, but the hoya annually produces delicate waxy flowers.

board or a piece of cork bark and hung. Some attention must be given to the root ball to keep it moist but not soggy. When the fronds appear to be thirsty, the entire plant plus its board or cork mount can be immersed in water until bubbles cease to rise from the center. Then leave it to drain and replace. Almost any fern usually grown indoors is satisfactory as a hanging basket subject, one of the best being the beloved Boston fern, *Nephrolepis exaltata bostoniensis*,

and its many varieties. The fronds of some species can be very large.

And perhaps the most charming trailer of them all is the little hearts entwined, *Ceropegia woodii*, with its trails studded with little gray-green heart-shaped leaves at intervals, looking almost as though they were moving about on feet.

Trees or shrubs

Probably the greatest number of indoor plants can be said to fall in this group, yet this is the broadest of collections, for although they may be tree-like or shrub-

In the foreground the soft, luxuriant trailers of a plectranthus make a solid but lightweight wall of color, while behind it the larger glossy green leaves of a *Philodendron bipinnatifidum* reach out on their long, arching stems.

like, they can differ widely in the size, shape, color and texture of their individual leaves. The familiar *Ficus elastica* and the tough little *Araucaria excelsa* are both trees but they are entirely different.

Most trees and shrubs are at their best when they are comparatively mature and large, for then they have a dignity, a presence and a definite function as a part of the room's decor. And this they most certainly can have, for they fill significant space and can therefore guide the steps in a certain direction or serve as a screen to give just a little added privacy to the corner of a room or office.

Because they are large, trees and shrubs can be used effectively in groups, for their individual shapes can be contrasted attractively one with another, and the shapes, textures and colors of their foliage in juxtaposition can be an exercise of careful and subtle choice.

Trees and shrubs useful as indoor plants include: *Brassaia* (syn. *Schefflera*) *actinophylla*, many of the large palms and bamboos, the tree-like *Pittosporum undulatum*, several of the larger philodendrons, podocarpus, some of the larger dieffenbachias, *Fatsia japonica*, the elegant *Dizygotheca elegantissima* and equally elegant *Ficus benjamina* or weeping fig, *Grevillea robusta*, and for limited periods and at certain seasons such splendid flowering shrubs as hydrangeas, camellias, azaleas, poinsettias and fuchsias.

Unfortunately, many people believe that bonsai or dwarfed Japanese trees are suitable for indoor gardening. This is not so. Bonsai trees are meant to be grown outdoors, not necessarily completely in the open, for most must have the shelter of some kind of light roofing and shading, but in an open atmosphere. Most can be brought indoors for a few days at a time and then taken out again, and if a number of bonsai trees are grown it is possible to have a succession of them on indoor display. Of course, it is possible to train certain house plants in the bonsai fashion, and while one may not have the authentic product, the plants will be perfectly at home indoors. A few plants being used for indoor bonsai are jade plant (*Crassula argentea*), Natal-plum (*Carissa grandiflora*) and various citrus.

Cocos weddeliana is a pretty little palm with dainty foliage that sometimes tends to go brown at the tips.

Several varieties of rubber plant have been hybridized. This all-green form is *Ficus elastica* 'Decora'.

Ficus lyrata has large, waist-like leaves, which have given it the popular name of fiddle-leaf fig.

47

4 Treatment

Watering

More indoor plants are killed by overwatering than anything else, perhaps because the basic function of watering is not properly understood. Water is needed by plants for two main and related reasons: (1) to keep the stems and leaves turgid so that (2) they can be fed with a constant stream of liquid food from roots to leaf tips.

Plant roots require both air and water, and when a pot is overwatered, all the air is expelled and the roots drown, rot and gradually starve the plant. Correct watering is a means of feeding the roots with both the moisture and the air they need.

It is impossible to lay down hard and fast rules about watering, for much depends on circumstances, weather and season. But it is safe to advise most strongly that no plant should be watered if the soil surface in the pot is moist. Let it get almost bone dry first. Plenty and seldom should be the aim.

With a new plant, for the first few times pour in water to the top of the pot and see if it gradually trickles out of the drainage holes in the base. If it does not, give it a little

Left: the leaves of most bromeliads form a vase or cup, which should always be kept filled with water.

more until it does, and try to bear in mind roughly how much water you gave it. Let the pot stand in the puddle it has made for about an hour. The soil may reabsorb this water, but if it does not, then empty it out. Never let any plant stand in water except such aquatic marsh plants as the umbrella plant, *Cyperus alternifolius*.

By watering in this manner you are moistening the whole of the root ball, not just a part of it, and allowing air to enter at the same time. The water in the top of the pot courses down through the spaces in the soil, pushing ahead the air within the spaces. As the water rushes downwards pushing the

An underwatered plant (*above left*) will eventually die because some of its roots are dry and cannot absorb food or moisture. Stale air accumulates to poison these roots and the soil cracks away from the pot

sides. When a plant is given too much water (*above right*) all the air spaces are filled and the plant cannot breathe. The roots become slimy, rot and fail to feed the plant with food or moisture.

An overwatered plant. Whether overwatered or underwatered, a plant will respond by drooping and, eventually, shedding its leaves.

'old' air ahead, it drags in new fresh air after it so that, like breathing, watering exhales the foul and used air and inhales the new.

Remember that it is always a simpler matter to add more water to a plant that needs it than to take away an excessive amount. A human being or an animal can choose how much to drink but a potted plant can only accept.

Since the symptoms of overwatering and underwatering are unfortunately almost the same, be cautious how you treat a plant whose leaves are drooping, yellow and tending to fall. Never give more water unless you are certain that the plant actually needs it, perhaps because you have been away, for example.

Plants in active growth under fluorescent lights, even in winter can use up large amounts of water. We know that plants require very much more water in summer than in winter, but watch the weather closely. A hot, dry day might also be dark, overcast and humid, in which case the plant is likely to lose only little water through transpiration. A hot, sunny day may cause some plants to wilt, yet their soil may still be moist. The answer to this is that transpiration is taking place more quickly than the plant can absorb moisture through its roots and the addition of water will make no difference. Instead, give the plant's foliage

49

a light spray of clean and tepid water. If this is impossible, remove the plant to a cooler or darker place, or draw the curtains for a little while.

Feeding

Enthusiasts will often overfeed their plants. This is bad for the plants and also bad for the owners, for if the plants survive this treatment they will grow large too quickly, outgrow their pots and become prone to disease.

Every newly bought plant probably has enough food in its soil to last at least 2–3 months and will not require feeding during this time. After this, feed the plant regularly according to season, but very lightly. Never for any reason exceed the quantities recommended on the bottle or packet. Far better to reduce the dosage slightly.

The kind of food or fertilizer you apply will depend on your personal preferences and their general availability. Fertilizers come as liquids, powders or pills. Plants can absorb foods only in the form of liquids in solution with the moisture around their roots, so obviously feeding and watering should take place simultaneously.

In winter, feeding should either be suspended entirely or its frequency greatly reduced depending to some extent on the conditions of warmth, light and water. In summer a very light feed once a week is preferable to a heavier fortnightly dose. Change from winter to summer treatment fairly gradually.

Fertilizers in pelleted form are pressed into the soil and gradually dissolve each time the plant is watered.

Spraying plants with a foliar feed has certain special advantages, for it helps to keep the leaves clean and gives a welcome humidity as well as providing food elements accepted by leaves as well as roots.

Left: powdered or granular fertilizers can sometimes be sprinkled on the soil and watered in, but are more usually dissolved in water and then added.

Above: all proprietary fertilizers require dilution and recommended doses should never be exceeded. It is easy to give too much liquid food, so measure quantities carefully.

The various foliar feeds available are useful but by no means essential. If it is inconvenient to spray the entire plant, remember that even foliar feeds can be absorbed by the roots of a plant, so consider using them as a normal fertilizer applied to the roots of the plant through the soil.

Not all plants need feeding through the soil, although this is normally where their roots and therefore their feeding system is to be found. The bromeliads, for example, have a shallow and comparatively unimportant root system, which would rot if continually fed. Most of them are epiphytes which use the branches of trees as support, collecting food from the leaves and other debris that might fall and attach itself accidentally to their roots. In their natural habitat bromeliads feed as they take in water from the central cups or vases formed by their leaf rosettes. But for the very occasional artificial feed they need, feeding through the soil will do as well.

Imaginative common sense is probably the best asset the indoor gardener has, but it is always advisable to check.

It is worth remembering that plants in our homes are influenced in their growth by the amount of light and warmth they receive. And this obviously has a great influence on the amount of food and water they require. If too much food and water is given, relative to the light and warmth, the plants soon become sickly. This, of course, adds a further complication to the problems of feeding and watering. Therefore, it is necessary to gain experience with your own plants and their requirements before buying very expensive and delicate plants. Careful observation is the true answer.

A further complication is that some plants have a resting period, and it is during this period that little water or food is required. These resting periods are often initiated in response to the temperature and light that is available, especially when nts are in their native habitats.

ortunately, the artificial conditions in the home often confuse the plants, and this sometimes makes it difficult to know whether to give or withhold water and food.

Group therapy

Growing two or more plants in association or creating a plant arrangement has obvious decorative advantages. Less obvious is the advantage to the plants themselves.

Most plants benefit from the close association with other plants just as they do in the wild. One plant helps to protect the roots constantly moist. There are two ways of making plant arrangements. The plants can be grouped together in their individual pots, placed together in a large bowl, planter or other container with the pots concealed with moss, fir bark, peat moss or pebbles. Or else the plants can be knocked from their pots and all planted together in a common soil inside the large container. Both methods have certain benefits. If the plants are kept in their pots, they can easily be taken out and replaced, while knocking plants from their pots does away with the problem of disguising their containers.

Plants grouped together in a mass can look effective if the collection has been selected with skill and the plants have similar food and water requirements.

other, and the combined moisture they transpire helps to create humidity and manufacture a micro-climate beneficial to the group.

So long as certain basic rules are obeyed a variety of plants can be grouped together. They should all require the same amount of moisture. It would be impossible to grow cacti with cyperus, for example, because the cacti normally need little or, at some times of the year, no water, whereas the cyperus is a bog plant that needs to have its

A compromise that gives the best of both worlds is to knock the plants from their plastic or clay pots and slip the root ball into a perforated plastic bag. This, being of negligible thickness and completely pliable, allows the plants to be grouped more closely together and yet remain potentially mobile.

Whichever method is used, special care

To make a bottle garden, first ensure that you have everything at hand. Check that the bottle is spotlessly clean and dry, for once work has started it will be too late to go back. Put a drainage layer at the base of the bottle. Use a light, open soil – sterilized so that no weed seeds will germinate. Grouping plants in a bottle garden demands an artist's talent. Look for contrasts in shape, color and texture but not of type, for all must live together under the same conditions.

will have to be taken to drain the large container that holds all the plants. If the plants are in their pots, it will be possible to control watering to some extent so that some plants get more than others, but there is always the danger that excess water from one might damage the roots of its neighbor. Plants out of their pots and in a common soil will obviously need some special provision for drainage, because in both cases the communal container may have no drainage holes. So for all types of plant arrangements it is essential to fill the bottom inch or so of the container with some draining material such as pebbles or pea gravel. At the same time, be sure to water with care, in the knowledge that any excess moisture cannot run away but will be contained in that basic drainage layer.

It is quite easy to plant a bowl or dish garden and to make a terrarium, and so long as the advice above is followed no real problems should be encountered. Rather more difficult is the creation of a bottle garden, where the opening or neck is too narrow to permit your hands to enter. The following suggestions will probably be helpful.

First make sure that the interior of the bottle is scrupulously clean before you begin and that it is completely dry. Pour in just a little peat moss through an improvised chute or funnel. This is mainly to break the fall of the next layer, the drainage

material, and avoid shattering the glass. This drainage layer should be fairly deep, preferably at least 2 in (5 cm). The soil, which must be sterilized to prevent weeds and must be sufficiently rich in plant foods to sustain gentle growth over a long period, should go in next. When inserting the soil through the chute, try to make sure that it does not soil the sides of the bottle, but try also to slope it a little or to make one or two hills in the soil surface.

The plants to choose for a bottle garden will obviously have to be small enough to enter the neck, so they will generally be immature. But the thing to remember is that they will grow. However, do not choose a subject that will grow either too large or too quickly, for in both these cases the plant will have to be severely cut down or removed completely to avoid damage to the other plants. Do not, for example, use creeping or trailing plants such as ivy or *Ficus pumila* unless you are prepared to trim them regularly.

The following plants are all suitable for a bottle garden: *Acorus gramineus* (grass), small-leaved varieties of *Begonia rex*, *Corex*

Attach any improvised tools securely to a slim cane.

Dig a small hole for the plant roots, being careful not to go too deep. Gently tease away most of the soil from the plant roots.

In order that the finished bottle garden can be seen clearly and enjoyed, the sides must be clean, clear and free from condensation. Water with great care and at long intervals for healthy and attractive plants – removal of unsightly elements is by no means easy.

japonica (grass or rush), *Codiaeum variegatum pictum* (croton), *Cryptanthus acaulis* (earth star), *Fittonia vershaffeltii argyroneura* (nerve plant – there is a dwarf form with very small leaves), *Maranta leuconeura kerchoveana* (prayer plant), *Chamaedorea elegans* 'Bella' (small palm), *Pellionia pulchra*, *Peperomia orba*. *Pilea cadierei* 'Minima' (aluminum plant), *Pteris ensiformis* 'Victoriae' (fern), *Selaginella*, *Sinningia pusilla* (dainty flowering plant only 1½–2 in (3–5 cm) high .

To plant out a bottle garden, tie a spoon securely to a long cane, insert it into the neck of the bottle and dig a little hole in the soil for the plant. Knock the plant from its pot, gently tease away some of the soil from its root ball, then, holding the plant by the tip of its foliage, insert the root through the neck of the bottle and lean the bottle so that the roots hang directly over the hole. Let it drop, use your spoon to move it to an upright position and then cover the roots with soil and firm. Repeat the process for the remainder of the plants. If you wish, you can add an occasional rock or piece of driftwood to dramatize the effect.

Add no more than a cupful of water, preferably sprayed directly onto the plants and soil, and also onto the inner sides of the glass bottle to remove any traces of dust or soil that may have been thrown up as work progressed. Theoretically, you can then

Below: two unusual and attractive containers suitable for similar gardens.

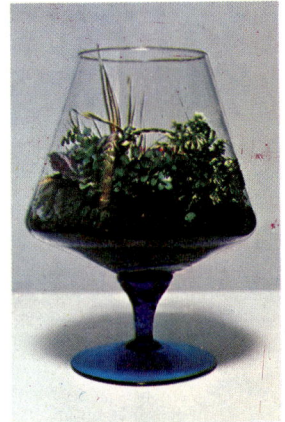

seal the top and the plants will grow for months without any further need for water. In practice, sealing the top nearly always leads to damping off, mainly because the balance of moisture to plant life must be exact. Compromise by watering sparingly,

Holding the plant by the tips of the leaves, position it and the bottle so that the roots will drop neatly into the prepared planting hole.

Spread soil over the roots and firm down.

certainly no more than once a month and in the smallest quantities. Keep the bottle garden out of direct sunlight and in a coolish position.

The growing of plants in groups in a container in the home dates back many years, to when in 1829 Nathaniel Ward, a London physician, accidentally discovered that plants could be successfully grown in a closed glass case. The water which evaporated from the leaves of the plants during respiration condensed on the glass and

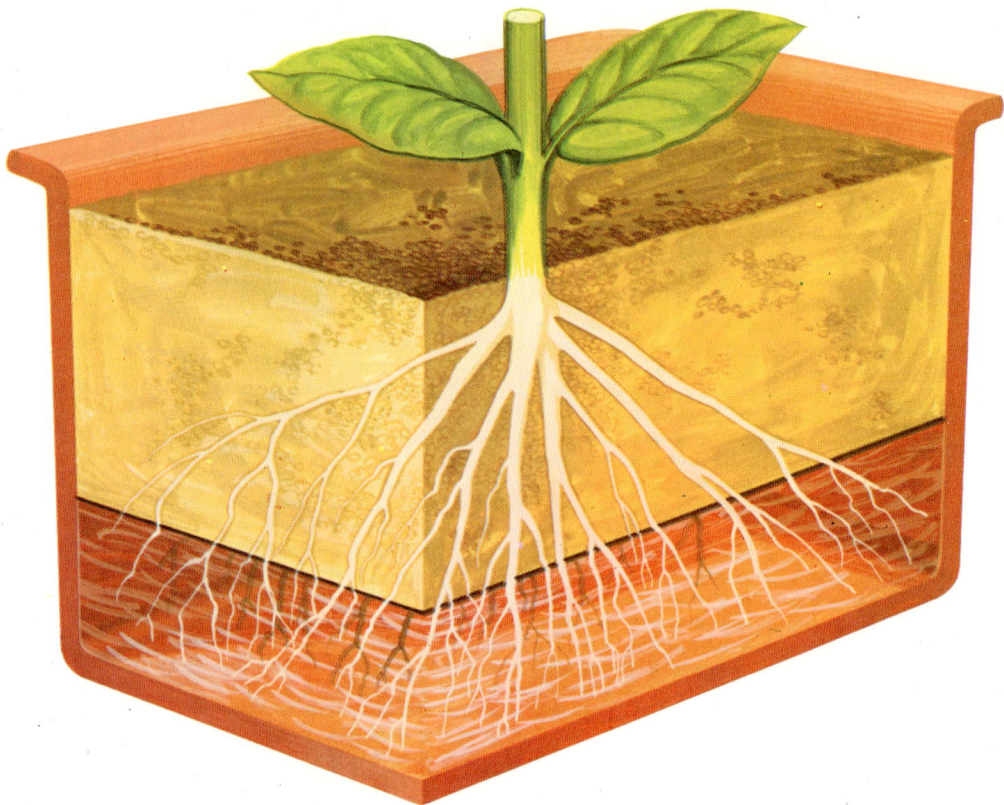

The growing medium of inert clay granules exists merely to anchor the plant through its roots, which serve also to absorb and distribute moisture, food and air.

trickled down the container's sides and back into the soil.

This idea was taken up by Victorian gardeners, who called these containers Wardian Cases.

Hydroponics

Paradoxical though it may seem, if you grow your plants in water only, the risk of overwatering vanishes. The roots are not merely submerged in water, but grow in a special medium that is kept moist from the water below. Thus they get moisture and air.

Although hydroponics, especially on a commercial scale, can become an involved process with sophisticated equipment and some knowledge of chemistry necessary for success, all this is only a somewhat expensive refinement of simpler means of growing plants hydroponically that have been used for many years. Without special containers, special growing media, special water-level indicators and special slow-release fertilizers, it is still perfectly possible to grow many types of indoor plants for months or even years at a time so long as one basic rule is observed.

The plant must rest in the neck of the container so that its roots can go down into the water and the upper portions of the plant grow upwards. Use a grid of wire mesh or something similar. The container itself should preferably be of glass so that the water level can easily and quickly be checked. The roots should be carefully washed clean of all soil and inserted in the container so that the plant is securely held in position. Water should then be poured in so that it covers all the roots. A touch of liquid fertilizer is added. The important point to remember is that to prevent the plant from drowning, the water level must now be allowed to drop, through absorption by the plant and by evaporation. This will mean that the roots are totally submerged in water only for a day or so, and then are gradually exposed more and more to the air, only the longer roots remaining below the water level. So long as these deeper roots still touch the water, the plant will receive sufficient moisture for its requirements, and so long as some of the roots are above water level they will receive sufficient air to keep them alive. Fertilizer applications should be regular but light.

A few plants especially suited to growing in water are: Chinese evergreens (*Aglaonema*), coleus, *Dracaena sanderiana*, *Fatshedera*, the heartleaf philodendron *Philodendron oxycardium*, common ivy (*Hedera*), *Scindapsus*, *Syngonium*, *Tradescantia*, *Zebrina* and of course the avocado and sweet-potato vine.

Many plants, of course, can be increased by immersing the cut ends of cuttings in water, where they will develop roots, but unless fed or potted into a compost they will eventually die. Cuttings of patience plant root easily by this method.

Water should be replenished to cover the whole root system only at moderate intervals, allowing the water level to drop considerably so that some roots touch water and some are in air. In the right-hand jar, the water level has been allowed to drop rather too far: halfway down is enough.

5 Propagation

Half the fun of indoor plants is growing your own, and with many plants this is a simple process. Some plants even produce their own young.

Although most indoor plants can be raised from seed, quicker, more certain results come from other propagation methods. However, if you have successfully started petunias, marigolds, tomatoes and eggplants (aubergines) from seed indoors, you can readily succeed with house plants, especially if you have a well-lighted room or lacking that, can supply fluorescent lighting. Selecting a plant that is quick and easy to grow, such as coleus, is recommended, but African violets and many other relatives among the vast gesneriad family also grow well from seed; others to consider are amaryllis, wax begonia (*Begonia semperflorens*) and some other kinds of begonia, impatiens, cyclamen, kalanchoe

A seed pan or pot in a sealed plastic bag is protected from cold and drafts. The seeds germinate safely and can then be gradually exposed to a normal environment.

and many cacti and succulents. Without the assistance of a propagating case and a greenhouse, the best means of growing seeds indoors is to make use of a translucent plastic kitchen bag.

Sow the seed in a moist sterilized growing medium in a pot or on a small tray and then place this inside a plastic bag. Blow into the bag so that the film stands clear of the soil surface and then securely tie up the opening so that the bag is virtually sealed. Keep the 'package' in the warm and watch carefully for the first signs of growth. If during this period so much condensation takes place that water collects in puddles inside the bag, open it, remove the pot or box, turn the bag inside out and replace the pot inside. As soon as evidence of growth appears, open the bag slightly, leaving the pot still inside. Remove the package from the warm location for a few hours each day, gradually lengthening this period and gradually opening the bag more and more until it can be removed entirely. When the little plants are large enough to be handled, carefully transplant them into individual pots, placing them under fluorescent lights or in a well-lighted location.

Plants can also be propagated by other measures.

Division After flowering, many of the exceedingly useful and decorative plants known collectively as bromeliads will produce a young plant growing from the soil beside the parent. It is a simple matter to cut away this young plant with a portion of root and to plant it in a separate pot.

Some plants such as aspidistras and sansevierias will produce more and more spiky leaves as they grow older and eventually these so overcrowd the pot that they should be divided. Again, merely knock the plant from its pot and divide the roots into portions, giving each a separate pot.

After some time the African violet will produce so many foliage rosettes that they choke the pot. Many of these are from separate plants, so once again knock the plant from its pot and very gently and carefully tease the tiny roots apart so that you get several plants. Pot these separately.

Cuttings There are several types of cuttings, of which the simplest is the method of propagating the ubiquitous tradescantia. Pinch out the growing tip of a long trailer and stick the end in a pot of soil; it will root almost immediately. Many indoor plants can be quite easily propagated with this type of stem cutting.

Leaf cuttings can be divided into several kinds. An African violet leaf, for example, with a tiny sliver from its stem, can be inserted in a pot of peat moss and sand and

When dividing the roots of a plant always make sure that each portion includes some good root hairs.

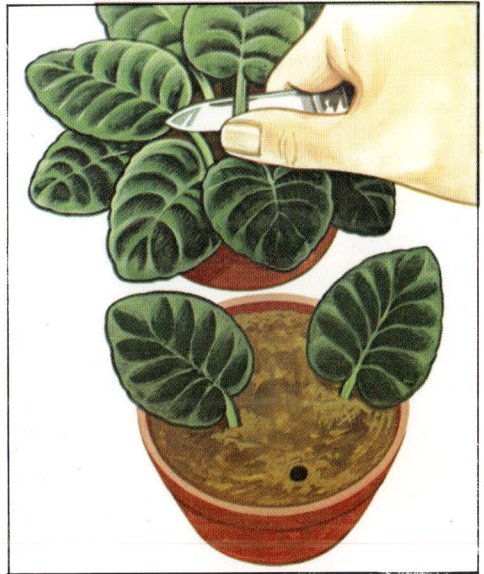

Bury the petiole right up to the leaf when taking leaf cuttings of saintpaulias.

Part of the attraction of a chlorophytum is the numerous long, arching stems bearing miniature plants at the tips.

To propagate a chlorophytum by layering, rest the plantlet on another pot of soil, if necessary holding it down with a hairpin, weight or toothpick.

will quickly take root. The long, spear-like sansevieria leaf can be cut into sections, each section planted in soil, and rooting will take place soon after. Many begonias, including *B. rex*, the ivy-leafed begonia, can be propagated in much the same way. Or by merely pegging a leaf flat to the surface of the soil and cutting through its major veins, new plants will be encouraged to root, which are subsequently potted up.

Layering One of the reasons for the popularity of the familiar *Chlorophytum comosum variegatum*, or spider plant, is its habit of sending out long arching stems, which first bear little white flowers and then miniature plants. If these are allowed to rest on the soil surface of another pot, they will quickly take root and can be cut from the original stem.

Most climbers can easily be propagated by layering. Take one of the stems or trailers and, a few inches (centimeters) from the growing tip, gently bend or twist the stem so that it fractures without breaking off. Bury this section in a pot of soil and after a time new growth will indicate that new roots have formed. Then cut the young plant from its parent. Trim back the shoot from the parent plant to avoid leaving an unsightly shoot.

pot up the young plant in the normal manner. Support the plant with a stake.

A surprising number of plants will send out roots if cuttings are merely placed in water. It is possible to make use of this characteristic to make a long-lasting room decoration for table-centerpieces and to grow a number of new plants at the same time. Take a fairly large waterproof container and cover the base with pebbles. Collect together stem cuttings from ivies, kangaroo vine and grape-ivy, tradescantia, heartleaf philodendron, impatiens or busy

Plant cuttings of many types will quickly take root if they are held by pebbles in a water solution. Make sure that the water level never drops too much for too long, or the plants will suffer.

Many plants, such as tradescantia, can be induced to grow roots if cuttings are merely placed in plain water. When the roots are well developed, remove the cutting and pot it up in a good soil.

Air layering It is obviously impossible to bend the growing tip of, say, a rubber plant, to layer it in the way described, but there is another method. Choose your spot a few inches from the growing tip and nick out a tiny sliver. Cover this with a good ball of moist sphagnum moss securely tied around the stem to cover the wound. So that the moss will not dry out too quickly, cover it with a piece of plastic sheeting firmly secured in place. It will soon become evident that roots will have grown into the moss. When this happens, cut away the top under these roots, remove the plastic and

Lizzie, coleus, peperomia or *Saxifraga sarmentosa* (there are many others), and insert these in the container, using more pebbles to secure the cuttings in place. Arrange them decoratively. Pour in water with just a trace of liquid fertilizer. Very shortly the cuttings will put out roots into the water.

When the plants have grown too large to remain together, pot them individually. This 'puddle-pot' method, as it is called, is a particularly easy and useful means of propagating several plants at once. Maintain a highish water level, but allow the roots to get some air occasionally.

61

6 Pests and diseases

So long as indoor plants are given the minimum of attention there is no real reason why they should suffer from any but the most superficial damage from pests or diseases. If they are kept clean, examined at regular intervals, maintained in conditions that are suitable for them, and not over-watered or overfed, most plants will live for years.

Examination is the real answer. Though one cannot subject every plant in the home to a minute appraisal every day, after a time even a casual glance will suggest when something is wrong; a twisted leaf, a yellowing, reddening or browning, a drooping – these are the primary signs of trouble.

Pests are far more likely than disease, and these are most likely to occur in summer or after plants have been brought indoors in the fall, rather than in winter. There is always the threat of attack from aphids coming in from the garden, normally quickly seen and as quickly settled. Red spider mite will attack only where the atmosphere is over-dry and arid. Less frequently, a tuft of white cotton will appear, indicating mealy bugs, or else a gray protuberance, which suggests scale.

Caterpillars, ants, earwigs, worms, slugs, thrips, white flies and other insects may also cause trouble, but none of these is likely to escape preliminary examination when a plant is first brought home.

Everything mentioned so far can be eradicated by a program of spraying with an insecticide such as malathion. This is a

Aphids can be brought into the home on garden flowers – or they may fly in through the window. They can be easily controlled by spraying with one of several proprietary insecticides.

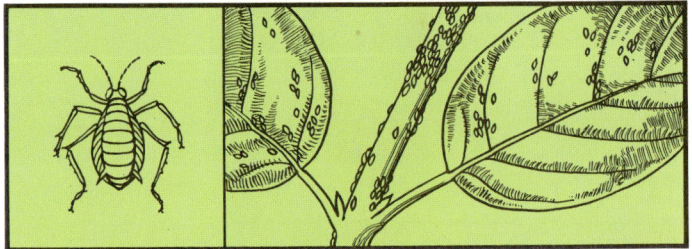

The almost invisible red spider mite attacks only when the atmosphere is dry and arid. Good humidity or an occasional spray will ensure that your plants are kept clear of this pest.

Mealy bugs are again almost invisible, but give themselves away by the white woolly substance with which they surround themselves. A drop or two of methylated spirits will kill them.

White flies can sometimes be difficult to eradicate, but a regular spraying with Resmethrin will do the trick. This is absorbed by the sap and then sucked by the insects.

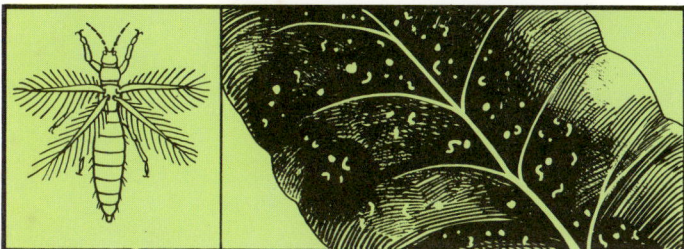

Resmethrin is also the answer to an attack by thrips – small black-winged insects that cause tiny pale spots on leaves where they suck the sap from the plant.

poison and as such it should never be used inside the house. Every plant to be treated should be taken out of doors and given a thorough spray, or even turned upside down and dipped in a bucket of the mixture as recommended on the label. Other sprays that can be used indoors will kill only mild infestations of aphids or similar pests.

Mealy bugs can be cleared safely and with little trouble by dipping a matchstick in alcohol and touching the white, woolly coating, which will then disappear to reveal the little brown insect within. Scale can actually be scraped off with a knife.

Red spider is a little different. It will appear only when the plant or plants concerned suffer from too dry and arid an atmosphere. It will be noted by a twisting, curling and drying of leaves and on examination it will be found that leaves are covered with a fine web in which move a great number of minute red-brown insects. Red spider mite can be cleared with careful and thorough application of most insecticides, such as malathion, but the best way of preventing a further attack is to increase the humidity by spraying the plant that has been affected. Sometimes a good washing of the plant's foliage at the kitchen sink will eliminate red spider mites and aphids.

There are very few diseases that attack indoor plants, and those that might appear are caused almost without exception by lack of care. If subjected to over-watering, for example, many plants can suffer from root rot, damping off, mildew or botrytis. Viruses and rusts can begin when a plant is sick through being kept too wet, too cold or both. If plants are kept in the dark or shade for too long, they will tend to become lank, weak and subject to disease.

Pests are, on the whole, a simple matter to clear, but diseases are more complex. They arise only after the plant has been seriously weakened. It is advisable to treat pest attack, but to throw the plant away if disease appears. You may waste considerable time and effort attempting to treat it and other plants may be affected.

If, on the other hand, a plant is so admired or so much a member of the family that every attempt must be made to cure it, a fungicide spray may help and, if possible, a period of recuperation in a greenhouse or plant room under ideal conditions.

It is better not to be too sentimental about indoor plants. Keep them while they are attractive and at their best. When they grow too old or become diseased – unlikely though it is – throw them away and acquire a replacement. This will be better and safer for any other plants you have.

Index